Numbering Our Days' Illusions

Also by Shanta Acharya

Not This, Not That
(Rupa & Co, New Delhi, 1994)

Shanta Acharya

Numbering Our Days' Illusions

Rockingham Press

Published in 1995
by
The Rockingham Press
11 Musley Lane,
Ware, Herts
SG12 7EN

Copyright © Shanta Acharya, 1995

British Library Cataloguing-in-Publication Data

A catalogue record for this book
is available from the British Library

ISBN 1 873468 34 2

Printed in Great Britain
by Bemrose Shafron (Printers) Ltd,
Chester

Printed on Recycled Paper

For my friends

*As the sun, the eye of the whole world,
Is not sullied by the external faults of the eyes.*

Katha Upanishad

Acknowledgements

Thanks are due to the editors of the following publications in which several of these poems first appeared, sometimes in different versions:

Acumen, Chapman, Critical Quarterly, Envoi, Feminist Arts News, Poetry Nottingham, Sheffield Thursday, Spokes Poetry Magazine, The Swansea Review, Wasafiri, Writing New Worlds (Pluto Press, 1995) in the UK.

Contemporary Indian Poetry (Ohio University Press, 1990) *The Journal of South Asian Literature* (Michigan State University) in the USA and *The Toronto South Asian Review* in Canada.

Chandrabhaga, Commonwealth Quarterly, ELT Forum Journal of English Studies, The Humanities Review, The Illustrated Weekly of India, Imprint, In Their Own Voice (Penguin India, 1993), *India International Centre Quarterly, Indian Literature, The Indian Literary Review, The Indian P.E.N., Indian Verse, The Journal of Indian Writing in English, The Journal of the Poetry Society, New Quest, Modern Poetry* (Oxford & IBH Publishing Co., 1977), *Poetry Chronicle, Tenor, Vortex* and *Youth Times* in India.

Contents

AFTER GREAT STRUGGLE	9
THIS OTHER SELF	10
LACKING A NADIR	11
KNOW THYSELF	12
A MOMENT'S OCCUPATION	13
NUMBERING OUR DAYS' ILLUSIONS	14
MEDITATION IN A BATHTUB	15
IN LISTLESS FEVER	16
SILENCE	17
SPEECH AFTER SILENCE	18
SECRETS	19
WISHES	20
PROMISE	21
SEARCH	22
ARRANGED MARRIAGE	23
HONEYMOON	24
ABSENCE	25
MORNING PRAYER	26
JOURNEY THROUGH THE MANDALAS	27
THE SELF ABSORBED	28
THE FACE OF BETRAYAL	29
THE DARK HOURS	30
NON MEETING	31
PARTING	32
BETWEEN US	33
MORNING THOUGHTS	34
YOU CAME TO ME, STRANGER	35
THE CHOICE	36
RESIGNED	37
THE PARTY	38
DAUGHTERS AND LOVERS	40
A KIND OF GOING HOME	42

THE SEAGULL	44
THE PART	45
CITY SLICKERS	46
CITY LIFE	47
ALL FOR LOVE	48
FOOL FOR LOVE	49
LOVE'S DELAY	50
LOVELAND	52
LOVE GAME	54
NAMES AS HOMES	56
LIVING ALONE	58
IT IS NOT	59
HINDU WOMEN	60
LOOSE TALK	62
SOMETIMES	64
ON REMEMBERING A NAME	67
FACING THE SUN	68
TOTEM OF A SUBTLER MOTIVE	69
HAVING SETTLED MYSELF	70
NOT ONE OF THE MYTHS	72
TOO MEAGRE	74
A GIDDY MANNEQUIN	75
NO LONGER DO I FRAME MYSELF	76
FREED OF FASCINATION	77
FRIENDSHIP	78
PYREXIA OF UNKNOWN ORIGIN	80
WAITING	81
TREES	82
FORGETTING	83
FOR THE DISPOSSESSED	84
WORDS AS PLACES	85
EYES UNREAL	86

AFTER GREAT STRUGGLE

After great struggle
descends
an alternative calm —

The mind's swirling sky
now emptied of its thoughts in snowstorm.

Wrapped up like Trappist monks
the trees preserve an immaculate silence.

The cold wind shakes
this proud stillness

Into crumbling flakes,
mercilessly
smiling at the helpless struggle

To keep up appearances at all costs.

Strange faces
sheathed
move in these streets

Wanting a more direct relation with the sun.

THIS OTHER SELF

I engendered out of me
this cognate other self
that I masquerade in.

Janus-faced, I can walk
like a column of sunlight
seeing everywhere these
passing days' play of mind.

I gave it to begin with
half of my powers so that we
could be truly schizophrenic —
like a long married couple
unable to love or hate —
with the hope of emptying myself of us.

It has grown in me
like a goliath of no-self
felling me to reign in me supreme.
After all, it is always myself.

LACKING A NADIR

Lacking a nadir
human relationships
scatter their dregs
somewhere in-between.

Subterranean flows
the indefatigable
impulse to be
a self alone

In the acquisition
of that corona
when identity
lies eclipsed.

I then escape
from selflessness —
the tyranny of tradition —
to the naked being.

This ruthless provocation
lies elemental beneath us all,
perpetual engagement
of disinherited self with Self.

KNOW THYSELF

The eyes take everything in,
snapshots of a chimerical world
through a filter of illusion.

So have I lost myself
beguiled by these pupils,
lenses that reveal me in each image,
as I focus upon, away from myself.

Know Thyself!

My only hope is to meditate
on my unexplored selves,
undiscovered continents;
unravelling the self's bag of tricks.

Determined to scale
the heights of self-knowledge,
plumb the depths of self-illusion,
I pass my days flourishing them with poetry.

A MOMENT'S OCCUPATION

Spread out alive as a river on arid soil,
I only wish to be perfectly empty;
to lie with my eyes turned upwards
in evacuation of all desires.

Suddenly, I am pitched into a whirlpool,
mounted on sense, arched in ecstasy,
churned in the trill of a moment's freedom.

In some distant angle
the sun bends the light on my vision
beyond a moment's occupation.

NUMBERING OUR DAYS' ILLUSIONS

Your flowers stand back in my bottle vase
precious like these hypocritical days
that depart silent, full of contempt,
offering a majestic ruse of vision.

I search for words on bright yellow
walls of sunlight that stand between us
every Sunday morning patiently watching
our shadows flow into each other.

We grow with the sun
numbering our days' illusions.

MEDITATION IN A BATHTUB

Condensation on the mirror
wipes me out of my orbit.

The rising steam of illusions
mould on the attic's ceiling.

Reflections blur the world escalated
with thoughts' unredeemable patterns.

I, lady narcissus,
seek only the unperturbed surface,
a clean, white, deadly mirror.

IN LISTLESS FEVER

In listless fever
I drift to your premises,
we each other's cognate
coalesce to one self.

You frame me in your mirror
static among the iris' monuments,
signalling to the surface
words trapped in our limbs.

Brief moments of sunshine
in the mind-blanched, winter-trees' sky
know the halcyon mural
that time sketched for us.

SILENCE

Like the eloquence of the figurines on Konarka,
like the inscrutable dialogue of the rainbow
that converses with heaven in one language
and the horizon in another, your silence speaks.

I too prefer the silence of the moon,
the silence of the inmates of heaven's harem,
the voluptuous stars.

Smiling at the fragmentary utterance of men,
memory only creates words out of memory
beguiling us with its repertoire of tricks.

If love chooses to be silent as eternity is,
will it signify anything else?
There is more poetry in a kiss
than in all the words that trade between us.

SPEECH AFTER SILENCE

After ecstasy you spoke stranger words
smashing silence into smithereens,
tiny purple spaces of amnesia.

Your voice in islands of silence
rehearsed intricate patterns of dying.

And your words in farewell,
birds of twilight in arabesque,
dislimn poems in retreat.

SECRETS

Secrets in me grow like trees
twisting roots
disturbing the harmony of soul.

Once again a landslide
of dreams spreadeagle
like a wild peacock's call.

Is it your silence still
residing on green boulders,
plain words, mossdecked ?

I shall wait for you to rescue
the immured images of myself
with the red-litmus-blue of childhood's dreams.

WISHES

If wishes were white steeds
I could've galloped
with my ten thousand thoughts untold —

Arrayed majestic
between the corners of my eyes
like the peacock fanned milky way —

To crossbeam the single stream from yours,
dark wells in emptiness,
spear-edged sunlight of sorrow.

PROMISE

Around the walls
of an ancient temple
you led me in ecstasy
carving words

Seven unredeemable times.

Your words
like the full-throated chant
of the Buddhist monks in prayer
rose to an immaculate crescendo

Showering me
with a spring harvest of silence.

SEARCH

Twenty three monsoons of my life
I searched for home,

Then learnt to suffer alone
the beating of a human heart.

Strange nights have known my disease,
loneliness that clings like sticking plaster.

With the rains, I too have felt
my uprooted-tree emptiness.

With the lightning
I have splintered my peace.

With you I floated merry paper-
boats down the youthful stream.

The boats flirted down the bend
dashing as I sat on turbid banks

Silently watching a lifetime of home-
sickness come avalanching down.

ARRANGED MARRIAGE

The bridegroom's profile
refracted through her purdah
of tears unused to the violence
of iconoclasm dressed as tradition.

That moment's reappraisal
warned her to faithlessness;
discard old ways for new,
worship new gods and shoes.

She was the arrow then
that darted forth from
the taut bow of culture into
the flaming pyre proclaiming

Impossible union with a stranger.
Love will rise like a phoenix, they said;
friendship will follow with the children of god.
But first one has to be turned inside out.

HONEYMOON

Afloat on a raft towed by dreams
we gushed down a wild river's course
with nothing much to hold on to
save perhaps the stars in our eyes.

Neither of us saw the storm
gathering in the horizon
that broke our homely raft in two.

With closed eyes he drank deep the honey
and left me with the cold platter of a moon.

ABSENCE

Spread against the damask-rose sky
my thoughts fly home,
white cranes into the sunset.

They have travelled in echelons
to melt into the twilight,
flaming satis in regal poise.

In your absence this sunset
is a funeral of dream petals,
a pyre stoked up with volatile promises.

MORNING PRAYER

She would repeat every word of his
framing each syllable in the curve of her lips,

Transcribing its history as the sounds
metamorphosed into the silence
that embalm her widowed world.

Her eyes would close enthralled
when her mind projected a new possibility,
an original relation between her self and his words

As if the right utterance of that breath,
with desirelessness, would resurrect her universe.

JOURNEY THROUGH THE MANDALAS

Mind in lotus pose
self-centred I sit
empress of my mandala.

Your unholistic eyes
immersed in duality
pierce mines of imperfection.

Spewing aureoles of doubt
your mind, snake-kissed, shines
with the thousand-petalled lotus.

Composed in surreal reverie
mind in corpse pose
I now lie, a hierological cipher,
empress of your mandala.

THE SELF ABSORBED

The self-absorbed narcissus at his pool,
you gazed into the stillness of my eyes
measuring the depths of your features.

These eyes are perfect mirrors
you cannot crack; their gilding
constantly repair your days.
It is your landscapes' river,
you said: aslant and refreshing
its nimble dialogues, reassuring
its currents for the leaping fish.

Engrossed you sit in the centre of this sanctum
pretending the pattern of our relationship
is just another artifice of vision.

THE FACE OF BETRAYAL

Tonight the storm howls my words back at me,
dead, mutilated like corpses.

Flashing lightning smiles of torture at me
like a mad scorpion lashing,

My truth thunders in a black pall of falsehood.

Pointing leprous fingers of contempt at me,
they screech with the frightened owl.

I have seen the face of betrayal,
cold, unfamiliar;

The glorious sunset fading.

THE DARK HOURS

I shun your shadow
as wailing of dogs
beneath my window in winter.

In the dark hours
blind flapping of wings;
the air fluttering wildly
with a haphazard moth's naivete
caught in the jaws of a lizard.

You eclipsed my sun
in your vast shadow,
clutching my sunflower world
in your faithless rapier fingers.

Heaped on the floor I lay
discoloured,
your cudgelled blows of deceit
convulsing;

Feeling deep the
deer against hound
in my marrow.

Look stranger,
you can hurt no longer.
The dappled moth escaped
trembling,
waltz-winged.

Sometimes, towards sunset
I watch the embers fade
the anger to indifference.

The moth shall grow wings to fly.
The sun shall open my sky.

NON MEETING

Our non-meeting is perfectly placed
in the intricate pattern of things
that have come my way.

We have at least been denied
the ordeal of small talk,
recovery of self from cliche.

Now we can create a common lexicon
for the escape of ourselves
in the style of Tajmahals.

PARTING

Had we known each other casually
like travelling companions
huddled in the same railway compartment
yet bound for different destinations,
this parting would not have been slow death.

Perhaps, we would have exchanged addresses,
passionately bartered promises;
at the eleventh hour, expressed
inexpressible sorrow
born of a moment's moment.

Then my face would have relaxed
into a kindly mask, poignant
after the initial distortions.

Back at home lighting the hearth
I would have broken the promises
to make a brighter fire burn.

After this long journey together
the moments chastely shared
like spangles of sunlight
suffuse eternity.

As my hand slips out of yours,
I seek life rushing past.
My eyes sadly watch the distances grow.

BETWEEN US

You spoke of space-labs and weightlessness,
I of inverted scars beneath the skin.

You concentrated on the stars
with laser beams in your closed eyes,
your head galaxies of void.

I offer you a poultice for your hurt.
But you tend to amputate emotions
with your rare chloroform intellect.

You've even dropped a few words
from your vocabulary of dying.

Life is a contusion,
you know as well as I do.

The winter fog only dishevels
the chaste memories of our passion.

And the morning sun grows on us
as the sea over studded shells.

MORNING THOUGHTS

This room is just too full of you
jostling with strangers I never knew.
Another morning descends in the hood of a magician
flourishing its wand to people my thoughts with you.

My body, a being apart,
with its supreme fact will not be lead.
It knows its premises better than I do.
Naked and sleep-heavy,
it responds to the cold damp in the air.

It is these morning thoughts' protean shapes
that oppress bouncing endlessly within these
walls transforming as I toss and turn.

I encounter new selves in your words
as I linger to hold fresh discourse.

The words begin to hurt fumbling thus in memory.
It is then I stumble across another fiction.
My body, silent and complete,
acknowledges it was never thus deceived.

YOU CAME TO ME, STRANGER

You came to me stranger with no questions on your lips.
I was silent too with the summer sun
Looking in at my door while I let you in,
Aware of the unanswered questions bristling in our situation.

You put aside strangeness arbitrarily.
Your eyes resolved peace against mine.
I trod cautiously, weary of detente, distrustful of words.

You offered me your story in the official leaves of a passport.
I fell for your daughter, now estranged from you,
Her ten years of innocence and a broken front tooth.
She cannot but reminisce what she once felt for you,
Now she may have forgotten your tenderness
As her mother did some years ago.

Memories surface consciousness for renewal
In the spray mist of dreams seeking birth.
You too diver, after you've gathered your armful of corals,
Will search for things unseen in this summer day's sun.

You might try to get in touch with me then.
You may never find the same person again.
But if you do come to me again, with no explanation
On your lips, I will be silent too with the sun
Looking in at my door while I let you in.

THE CHOICE

1

My mind imagining itself
a shaft of sunlight
refracted in your medium.

With my several selves
I folded myself into your body,
content to be a colourful crowd,
celebrating in your prismatic streets
for a frail moment only.

I never begged eternity or your soul
but for myself the choice to be free;
a promise given at the beginning of time
to let the sunlight play in our streets.

2

This present fiction is of my mind.
A familiar pain trails the mind's creations
released in what-might-have been.

Realigning forces I emerge the same;
out of myself endlessly emerging
to surprise your fragmented selves
though destined to miss you.

My body, cold and critical,
stirs to draw the curtain
and let the sunlight stream in.

RESIGNED

Naked I came
reduced to my alphabets
like a tree striving to be a seedling
and tried to confess all

Through shifts in our stances of embracing,
twitching of finger-ends and eyes crossing.

Finally, having been failed by all,
all my words and yours and our touches,
I resigned to be dumb and unmoved, and

Let what is being be.

THE PARTY

1

Fashioned to have so much and no more,
trained words from suave lips that spat laughter
flowed civil from his bachelor figure.

He spoke of death that robbed a mother of her son
while she imagined an aeroplane somersault in the sky
before diving aflame to the earth. This burning
of the dead threatened to consume her so.

Her intent gaze nodded concession to desire
that scorched him while he hovered in distant circles
thinking she could remain familiar yet unscarred.

All was still; the sky was a blaze of colours.
He opened a window in the room, the air tensile.
She was flushed yet retained her tentative calm.

The night discovered a birthday person;
with Beethoven and Mateus Rosé they buried the dead

He had been trailing her orbit long
waiting for one such day to come.

2

When the sun appeared the next morning
she was his; his limbs encircled her, satisfied.

His brain judged every movement of her body,
the way her skin shone, the walls of her stomach
caved in and how her body was finally mastered;
failing to discern the direction of her thoughts.
The violence of his thoughts blotched the sun.

While she drew him into the vortex of her person,
the further back he crouched in his dark, separate thoughts;
a brittle, no-feeling glaze in his eyes and touch
after he had lunged into the eye of the sun.

She suffered the indifference of his withdrawal
before the sun could rise on her sighs.
His words continued to stab at her,
aware that his empire had fallen
even before it was begun.

She froze under his touch, but soon
splintered the ice with her laughter;
her dreams blew up in flames
with the longings of the sun.

DAUGHTERS AND LOVERS

1

Cordelia could not heave her true heart into her
mouth even for her fond and foolish father.

Lear had loved her most, but in a moment's
reversal disowned her without any dowry,
without his grace, his love, his benison;
becoming thus the natural fool of fortune.

He went to night school in the storm on the heath
with a fool, a follower and a madman.
Lear learnt quickly: "Is man no more than this ?
A poor, bare, forked animal as thou art?"

But the worst was still to come
for Lear was King Lear still:
"I am a very foolish fond old man."
Carrying his dead daughter in his arms,
his poor fool hanged, fools both of fate;
fools of the god of human nature.

Like a tired child on stage,
Lear went to sleep with Cordelia in his dreams.

2

Enter Hamlet musing to himself:
To be, or not to be — that is the question...

Ophelia appears thinking that Hamlet's love
for her is the reason for his distraction.

In two simple sentences he confirmed her suspicion —
I did love you once. And then — *I loved you not.*

His solution for her was sincerely meant:
Get thee to a nunnery;
why wouldst thou be a breeder of sinners?
A self-obsessed mind holding the mirror
to his cracked image of himself.

Hamlet's self-knowledge was all his own
It was not something that Ophelia could glean.

If thou wilt needs marry, marry a fool;
for wise men know well
what monsters you make of them.
To a nunnery, go...

How now Prince, was that wisely
spoken to true Ophelia ?

Orphaned and spurned by her Prince Charming;
drowned, nor knowing if she was loved or not:

Ophelia died without any such illusion.
It is the sort of thing that lovers do.

A KIND OF GOING HOME

For one precious, unforgettable day
you were loaned to us, only to be taken away.

I knew you not but like a shaft of light
you penetrated my inner emptiness
making me look unsparingly upon your death
as a kind of going home.

After months of preparation for your homecoming,
for the safe, though premature, arrival
of their dreams sublimated in your fragile body;
your parents never for one instant
admitting any impediment in welcoming you
home as the heart of their family.

In the beginning, when you kicked and frolicked
exploring the limits of your navigations
inside the high seas of your mother's womb,
we monitored your progress introducing ourselves
as you levitated saintlike in your space capsule.

Considering how everything that could go wrong, did go wrong,
your clear rejection of our world makes perfect sense.
You left a mother shorn of her dreams, bereft of hope,
and a father confounded not knowing how exactly to cope
with the permanent nature of your departure,
knowing of no fit ceremony to reconcile dreams with reality.

Your brief sojourn unleashed a groundswell of emotions
darkening earth and sky into one granite ocean of confusion
after your exit banished rationality out of fashion.

I do not know what you looked like
when they set their weary eyes upon you
struggling for your life in an incubator.
I can only see their faces, cadaverous masks —
of your father, my brother; your mother, my sister-in-law —
frozen in incandescent grief, their expressions raw
like a Francis Bacon painting, horror contained,
depicting human tragedy overwhelming for any philosophy.

THE SEAGULL

The story begins with a teacher,
Medvedenko, in love with Masha
who is in love with Konstantin
who is in love with Nina
who loves Trigorin, a minor
novelist in love with himself.

Trigorin is also loved by Arkadina,
an actress, the mother of Konstantin
who is in love with Nina-in-love-with-Trigorin.

In one inspired moment,
Trigorin tells Nina a fable
about the shooting of a seagull;
about a man who meets an innocent girl
like Nina, near a lake in the country
and quite idly destroys her.

Nina does not listen carefully to his story
nor does she think before she leaps into his arms.
Nina wants to be an actress and Konstantin a writer.
Both ruin themselves and each other
cocooned in their world of illusions.
He continues to love Nina and she continues to love Trigorin
Trigorin continues to love everybody but mostly himself.

Nina calls herself the seagull that Konstantin
had shot casually. Konstantin never deciphers
what she means. In one distracted moment
he kills himself just as he had shot the seagull.
And, thus mercifully ends a tale of unrequited love.

THE PART

Expelled from my mother's womb,
I fell into this world without aplomb;
my entrance into this wonderful stage
was not accompanied by the usual damage
that life tends to serve in generous portions.

Once admitted, like a stage prop, I have played
my meagre part to the best of my ability.
It is the role that is at the heart of my discontent.
I have watched others with lesser talent
being groomed for the prized part.

Can I appeal for surely my role is miscast?
I have the genius, I await the part!
How long must I wait and watch from the wings,
pretend I have no art, the conceit of humility,
the penance of watching others murder each act?

The clear light of intellect is no recompense
for such injustice, nor a forthright heart.
No explanation exists in the random distribution
of the gift of the alchemy of life's coveted parts.
I want to create my unique role but end up
watching destiny play its inimitable part.

CITY SLICKERS

Helmeted musclemen gliding on steel escalators
bomb-proof buildings in the City against terrorists.

Space-walking on huge walls of glass,
they examine me as they would any other lass.

Smiling, they take a random walk, unafraid of vertigo
like the stock market index raring to go.

Who said men do not make passes at women with glasses?
Real men do, particularly at women in City offices!

Cubicles, now shatterproof, hold fragile egos.
Men in dark grey suits shuffle in corporate shoes.

Pin-stripe suits come and go, talking of P/E ratio,
top-down, bottom-up methods of the intelligent investor.

As I mend the rules of the old boys' network
and demand my share of the profits of my work

I hit the invisible glass ceiling each time
I stand up for myself as if that was a crime.

A single Indian female, I am trapped, alas,
in a cage of bomb-proof, shatter-proof glass!

The Jurassic laws in the City continue to spawn
dinosaurs that even a Spielberg cannot improve upon.

Next time these helmeted musclemen blow me a kiss,
I will signal to them to rescue a woman in distress.

CITY LIFE

Getting up early, having gone to bed late
is City life; in between work, there is no respite.

Markets keep the adrenalin flowing, giving life a *buzz;*
but these whizz-kids are no match for the wizardry of Oz.

Analysts, brokers, consultants, directors of companies
advise me about investment themes and theories.

I organise company visits hoping to meet the ordinary
worker on the floor but that is not deemed necessary.

Dressing in colourful suits, not the bland City grey;
I commute on the misery line for my karma every day.

Unskilled in the art of self-promotion, the rat race,
I fail to flatter the fragile, feckless egos of my bosses.

I watch myself drifting sideways in organisations
with my mind moving laterally in new formations.

While excelling in my job as a stock picker,
I confound myself in my poor investments in a partner.

I have thus mastered the art of winner loses all
for not everything that goes down reverses its fall.

Nor do things I give boomerang back to me
in equal measure for then life could be *mon ami.*

Living alone, I try not to become the weekend worrier.
I can't see the future through a rearview mirror.

ALL FOR LOVE

Whose fault is this that the one I adore
is in love with someone else,
and I'm not in love with the one who worships me
but continue to love him who loves me not?
This one-way traffic does not make much sense!
God, how did I get into this madness?

I'd like to believe in God's omniscience.
The thought itself is comforting,
not a blade of grass stirring
nor even a poor sparrow falling —
you know, that sort of thing —
without some divine plan being fulfilled!
At least, it takes the weight off my shoulders.

But, honestly I fail to see
how my loving you and you loving her
is going to help anybody in anyway?
I doubt God's purpose is served in that!
Perish the thought, but if she whom you love
is in love with someone else instead of you
what a fine mess that will be?

But where do I fit into all this?
It is not quite an eternal triangle
nor a chain of love but a haphazard queue
which I'm reluctant to join.
I'm not exactly skilled in
experimenting with the joys of love
in three dimensional relationships.

I will walk down the straight,
though not narrow path of my life,
recovering my sanity with fellow illusionists

who like me bartered reason for love's ecstasy;
fools for love, willing victims of its magic.

The lonely trek from the heights
of Himalayan pleasure to the dry plains
of common sense is revelation enough.
Only brave explorers get there in the first place
unafraid of loneliness if the venture fails,
gamblers willing to risk all for love!

FOOL FOR LOVE

A fool for love, a pawn in the hands of destiny,
I have spent a lifetime accommodating ignominy.
Having short-changed myself for that rare coin,
I await for a tip from fickle love and recognition.

Nobody said it must be so; I laid down the rules myself.
Time to move on, I reckon; create a fresh game plan
for the party goes on, the music never ceases,
only brief pauses with new players and different rhythms.

In the game of musical chairs in life as in love,
once you are out, nothing is to be gained through analysis.
Love like history rarely repeats itself
and when it does, you don't have the wisdom
to recognise that such is the case.

In this love bazaar where goods cannot be purchased duty free
there is a high price to be paid for each gift.
You'd better be rich if you're planning a spending spree!

LOVE'S DELAY

Whatever makes you tick
also makes you unique.
If you let me share
your private fantasy,
you admit me inside your skin
letting me wander where nobody else has been
to discover just what makes us tick
what makes you and me, together, unique.

Loving is about giving,
giving at the right time
without holding back,
naturally, like leaves
growing on trees in spring;
giving freely all of oneself
for loving is about surrendering
oneself without restraint
as the love that I now seek hopes
to find me at the precise moment of my need.
Our mutual desire to give, to receive must coincide.

Love's delay means that you are not
ready to allow me inside your skin.
You flee like a male seahorse from danger
flashing amber yellow as a caution light,
changing hues from drab to neon,
indicating clearly your uncertainty
your unpreparedness to accept responsibility.

I read your mind like the mercury in a thermometer
adjusting my desire to reflect
fully your emotional temperature.

Loving is about waiting,
sometimes for a very long time,
without demanding anything,
not even an explanation;
it is about total abdication of power
for the love that you will need later
may not be there at the moment of your need.
Our mutual desire to give, to receive may not coincide.

What chance has our love of synchronising this ?
Love's delay may not always be amended with a kiss.

LOVELAND

Next time I find myself in loveland where everything
seems and nothing is quite what you think it to be,
I will be prepared too with my magical spectacles,
ready to participate in the carnival with my mask.
I will be different and not make silly mistakes,
I will be as wise as the wizard of Oz!

Give it enough time, things will start to go wrong
even in loveland,
          and I will make the same mistakes as we go along,
not in a recognisable pattern, that would be too easy to discern;
love knows when one journey has ended and another begun.
Even a child with no knowledge of love understands
that getting what one wants is not a game of abacus.

There is no advantage in matters of the heart
with years of experience, wisdom and all that crap.
I can still make a fool of myself, a jaded joker,
and transform this crying game into a laugh.
Love like death, equalisers both, doesn't respect pride;
it's a land where discrimination never trespassed.

Loveland is where you wander freely, with no documents,
no passports, no visas, no curriculum vitaes,
with nothing to declare but yourself without ever being asked
in confidence, in reverence, as in one's prayer,
a confession to the one who has conferred such freedom;
except that it's a land of myths, make-belief and legend

Where the face of the beloved remains the same
though the bodies keep changing with time and place;
everything seems the same but nothing is really the same,
only time passes, even that is difficult to decipher
for one is looking at the lover's mask in a trance.
It is a country where you never tango with reality.

Next time in loveland I will regard all ceremony
with the hope of being enlightened with love's epiphany.

LOVE GAME

When two individuals meet
and the chemistry is right
for friendship and love and more,
or whatever the final score;
they consent to play a complex game
with two sets of jigsaw puzzles
of each other's identity
except that the pieces are all part
of the other's chameleon personality
and one is expected to assemble
an image of the other
with one's capacity to feel,
to sense and to know the other
like a game of chess being played
by the imagination alone
but the game is not to checkmate
your partner but to anticipate
every word, action and thought
picking fragments that fit into place,
the pieces finally beginning to make sense.

In their efforts to identify what they love,
two friends help create the lover in the other.
Often the essence is discarded or simply lost
for one cannot construct the full image ever.
It is simply a process of intuitive selection
better known as self-preservation.
So when I create you, I create what I love;
the rest I leave as excess baggage in life's journey
hoping that life will not compel me later
to put all of a lifetime's pieces together.

I may not have the courage or the desire
to take a good look at all of myself or you

but if I can create as complete a picture of you
(knowing that time is the best artist of all)
and you attempt to do the same of me
with a lot of help from each other,
we stand a pretty good chance of never
having to fall out of love with each other.
That is why I am content
to let us take that bit longer
than is customary in delicate affairs of the heart
to get our jigsaw puzzle fit right from the start!

NAMES AS HOMES

What's in a name? You jokingly quote the bard.
Everything! Take mine, for instance:
"Shanta Acharya," I introduce myself
and the faces suddenly go blank,
not the oriental sort that reveals nothing
but a western impasse that conceals nothing!

I try to connect and negotiate
as I underplay my embarrassment.
"Do you remember how The Wasteland ends? Shantih?
Shanta is the same word, meaning peace,
and Acharya refers to the enlightened one!"
The exercise is only meant to break the ice,
makes a change from talking about the weather.

Most people reckon it is an Indian sort of name
even though they can't pronounce it.
They enquire politely which part of India I'm from.
After all, it passes the time in a civil way
and I do have a pan-Indian sort of name and face,
quite difficult even for an Indian to guess!

When I say Orissa, you hear Mauritius
and recognition flickers across your face.
I feel guilty of having to deny you that much success,
but having lost our way all over again,
we are on another journey through unfamiliar terrain.

I try a simpler route to explain:
"It is south of Calcutta."
What's a few hundred miles between friends?
That usually works, thanks to Mother Teresa
and the others who have laboured
to put Calcutta in the map of the world.

And, if I really want to expand your mind, I add:
"If you draw a horizontal line from Bombay,
across India, it will pass through Bhubaneswar,
the capital of Orissa, in the middle of the east coast,
south of Bengal and north of Andhra Pradesh!"
I grow into that dot in the atlas of the earth.

While it takes me two days to travel
from Bombay to Bhubaneswar by train,
we get somewhere over a drink in one evening.
My history and geography remain the same,
and I retain my name like an ancestral home.
So, you see my friend, there's a lot in a name.

LIVING ALONE

Living alone abroad confers one with a certain
flexibility of vision; I am anglepoised on
the inanities of custom and tradition.
I mix and match my moods with life's concoctions.

I dress contrary to fashion and sleep as much as I wish
and live like a nun as I have yet to meet my prince.
I do not read the Sunday papers nor watch TV in bed;
my thoughts are all my own, not influenced by anyone else!
I dislike parties and rehearse growing into an old maid.

When sad, I play my eclectic music full blast
and furiously clean my immaculately clean flat!
I switch on my answering machine to relax
in my perfumed bath, surrounded with incense and candles;
sipping chilled vodka from a crystal glass.

If I need to think in peace, I go for a long walk
in Hampstead Heath, Highgate Cemetery, or Waterlow Park.
London's theatres, concerts, operas and art galleries
dispel my periodic sense of claustrophobic unease.

When happy, I direct dial my parents in India
lingering in their garden of love like a butterfly,
I pray that the thunderstorms of life pass me by.
Living alone abroad, I have learnt to sense danger
in people unable to control their greed and fear.

I make albums and videos of my travels around the world,
immortalising a smile, a look, a shake of the hand
with strangers unafraid of contact. Living alone abroad,
I hoard memories to see me through when I am old.

IT IS NOT

It is not when you are coming to meet me
with my eyes anxiously waiting to cast their net in yours,
my body pitching all the colours of your mind
arched in ache like a quivering rainbow taut
across your skies of casual encounters

But when I am turning away, alone,
tired not with what you give, but what you deny
for the lack of which are we both unredeemable;

No longer grappling with the inane art
of naming things and then deconstructing them,
only being in one corner of consciousness, subliminal:

You will, perhaps, discover that love is.
I am not even sure that is the name.

HINDU WOMEN

In the Hindu niche of my heroines gallery
hang some exclusive miniature portraits,
top girls worshipped in their country.

Savitri is one whose puja is strictly done by my mother
paying her homage to the sati's indisputable power
in renegotiating the lease on the life of her husband
from repossession by Yama to populate his land.

Then, there's Sita's story to marvel upon.
After twelve years in exile from home and throne,
not to mention the ordeal of being courted by ten-faced Ravana,
Sita was expected to defend her chastity,
in a trial by fire as decreed by some committee.
Much too embarrassed of her own husband and king Rama,
she prayed for the earth to protect her honour.

Miraculously, mother earth did rise to the occasion
and sheltered Sita from the ignominy of such purification.
Imagine Sita's expression as she bowed out in style —
relief, surprise, pride, sorrow, loss, vindication —
all captured in her face, struggling for domination.

Draupadi, a free spirit, chose Arjuna in a swayamvara
and unwittingly acquired five husbands to protect her.

So she thought until pawned away by the five-headed Pandus
in a drunken game of dice loaded with their lost honour.
Humiliated in public, she escaped being stripped naked
by the shameless Kauravas, sheathed in her magical sari.

Parvati is also called Durga or Kali.
Being wedded to Shiva,
the creator-preserver-destroyer of the universe,
makes her feel schizophrenic.
As Kali, she is formidable in her garland
woven from her victim's heads;
As Durga, she smiles on all creatures
in a gesture of marvellous apotheosis.

Radha with Krishna remain at the centre
of this mandala with their song and dance,
their legendary love and romance.

Laxmi and Saraswati are my favourites.
Laxmi, goddess of wealth and success,
Saraswati, goddess of knowledge and the arts;
they reach out to my inner recess.

Often merging in my dreams into one female entity,
they shower me with life's redeeming multiplicity.

LOOSE TALK

You can hold your peace all on your own
if you can learn to hold your tongue.
This was sound advise from my grandmother
to her daughter. And, if anything is not
to your liking, it is best to take the name
of the Lord, Hari Om, for that is not in vain!

My tongue-tied grandmother so loved my mother
that she gifted the treasures of her wisdom to us
in our ancestral home as we shared her legacy.
My mother taught me yoga as a child,
how to arch like a bow, raise my body like a snake,
roar like a lion or stretch my tongue as far as my nose.

I encouraged her to loosen her tongue
for it was her story that I yearned to hear
in her words, unfurling like the national flag
on Independence Day to the anthem that we sang together.
My mother's tongue is Oriya —
mysterious as lake Chilika and lyrical as Konarka.

But I grew up living my life in English,
inhabiting words that have become my own,
colours that have mingled into a richer shade.

How can you hold my worlds apart
even if you deny me my runaway tongue?

Critics, like ruthless children, pelted my snake-
tongue which had not learnt to rattle.
In a world devoid of plainspeak, I sought
remedy from my gods: *Hiss, child hiss!*
And I graduated from an obedient lisp
to shedding my shame and singing my song.

Delivering reminders of the power of my tongue
swaying in rhythm, balancing on cobbled words,
at one moment a himalayan avalanche,
at another, spouting lava from my guts,
ripping earth and sky in one graceful stroke;
I am mistress of my tongue.

Cryptic and monosyllabic,
I learnt to be like the sphinx.
Straight as an arrow, brief as a haiku,
I laboured to create the pearls of wisdom,
with years of devotion, thus coming
full circle to my grandmother's home-truths.

With tongues of fire must I speak
for grandmothers and mothers in silent revolt,
daughters and sisters, all striving to sing one story,
variations of a similar fate.

SOMETIMES

People change, and smile; but the agony abides.
                                             T.S. Eliot

1

Sometimes, when the nights are long
and my thoughts are empty,
full of the silence of words
never meant to be spoken;
I know in the darkness
between us nothing can be over.

I look through the curtains
for the stars, lest they disappear
in this torpid air of disaffection.

Sometimes, when I am
completely at peace with myself
curled in waking en route to my dreams,
I know there wasn't anything we could do.

I walk past all our celebrated ways of knowing
into my innermost temple where you sit.
I confess to you how broken I am,
how frail without you these hours of my self.

Sometimes, in my sleep
when I wake up howling,

dreaming of myself drowning
in some unknown seas; of wars
strangely enough in our own streets;
my mother lonely near the stained-glass window,
her thoughts incandescent in silence:
my tears seek your touch alone.

I search for you in these lingering hours
remembering how we embraced the time you said:
This is the most permanent thing in the world.
I emerged pure as the ritual.

2

You always preferred silence
refraining from words to fill me
with your infinite loneliness.
At a touch of your hands a whole new
view of the world passed into my mind.

It is not as if now you are silent
even though I may pretend it to be so.
Your absence hurts me like your words
that having lived in this room know
just how I poised as a wave ready
to break on your eager shores.

Sometimes, you loved me too
with all your loneliness, your silence.

With the gift of this silence
I carve these words for you;
our relationship wanted not the intensity
but a certain fullness of expression.

There is perhaps no use in trying to look
at such things later as we can't retreat in time.
Every new relation is a new word
struggling against silences to come.

I no longer await your unpromised return
nor am I certain that this spring's flowers
will be less fragrant without you.
I am not even sad that my love
could not entirely contain you.

If you were to come back to me,
I would quicken each pulse in you
and from freedom set you free.

3

Sometimes, when I think I had
given you all, that you turned
aside full of me and all I offered,
I breathe solitude none can share.

Knowing it not, whatever one desires
one is; knowing is all.

ON REMEMBERING A NAME

*She would talk a little to herself as she combed her hair
Repeating his name with its patient syllables,
Never forgetting him that kept coming constantly so near.*
                                            Wallace Stevens

Is it your name that approaches
without you, interminable adventurer?
There is always something moving
in the memory of your name.

I can even preserve my footsteps
within its sacred space.
Your name is not to be profaned
when I hold durbar of all my selves.
The repeating of your name even focuses
the edges of my blurred and frayed self.

The syllables in orchestral shapes
appear tenderly gleaning my days.
It is a useful swastika at the precipice of memory
whirling me straight into the eye of my loss.

FACING THE SUN

Dying roots facing the sun
endure a felled-tree dumbness
long after your words struck the axe
in heaving me out of my centre.

My leaves clutching the earth
hear the hooves of words retreating.

I never anticipated this spoliation of self
from the elusive encounters of our knowing
that admitted only a moment's tethering.

You too never reckoned such leafing,
recompense shimmering green in the sun
before you began this felling.

Here, then my necessary defoliation
to overcome a majestic ruse of vision;
the disjointed centaur of your stance,
now familiar your routes of escape.

Rising among the shadows of your words
are shapes that you keep slaying until
your words are no longer travelling echoes.

This uprooted-tree ambience once breathed,
my unspoken words spangle the sun.

TOTEM OF A SUBTLER MOTIVE

Totem of a subtler motive, your affected reserve
abashes the reckoning of the Judas-kiss
with the memory of an ancient wound scabbing.

Slowly the scowl smothers itself with the pain;
recognition enlivens the still, smouldering face,
ice thaws on your expressive contours in flame.

Your words gushing forth refine their sartorial grace,
fashioning the elusive robes of each passing day.

All this is supposed to leave me a guaranteed gem.

A faceless victory you seem to have culled
in hoisting me like Caesar's trophy, without finesse.

Once profaned, the beautiful icons disappear
with the re-enactments of a half-faithful caring.

Time carries all our defences away,
guileless as a child retrieving its armful of toys.

Triumphalism rolls through the incubus
dragging me with my tiara of words.

HAVING SETTLED MYSELF

Having settled myself
into this mutual infidelity,
concert appears not
the sole valency of strength.

Did you think it strange
that we should be devoured
by a lie that spreads through
our words and smiles ?

Truth comes in strokes of pain.
We compose in vain the broken refrain
of a song no longer sung from the heart.
Living consists in
procuring temporary anodyne.

Having mastered the reflexes
of such an inner writhing,
knowing we could never pitch the abyss;
our saturnalia is destitution of faith.

In mutual recrimination
we align in our confession,
irreversible this slow sclerosis of breath.

At intervals I stop to scorn
my own paltry performance;
weary of charades and artefacts,
recognising the need for all that.

I can no longer live disinherited
in your gilded world
of convertible bonds and champagne.

It does not take much to keep intact
the integrity of one's self; that much I can state
for a fact having settled myself into this and that.

NOT ONE OF THE MYTHS

Not one of the myths we make
will outlast the muting of our breath.

What comes and goes in silence
represents time's landscape of self.

So long estranged from my self,
I have created an illusion —

Carefully camouflaged
to welcome our re-entrance.

It is like passing from the object
to its unredeemable shadow,

Like leaping off the canvas of a painting
into the gallery of free spectators

Only to dread that moment of return
to another image that would recapture us.

A plastic version of all that passed among us
or others who unknowingly resembled us.

The imageless wind is the appropriate conception,
projecting the naked self, the final relation.

There arrives a time when the fiction is a mirror
image of itself; a thing final in itself.

Unable to discern between illusion and creation,
we have stopped revolving in self-abnegation.

After the wind has gathered its unique composure
and we breathe deeply the pure, fulfilling air

Our halcyon gestures resurrect words from silence
like conjurors revelling in tricks and games.

The myths dissolve in the silence that guts
our ineffectual, self-mutilating words.

TOO MEAGRE

Too meagre it was to die for you,
letting myself down in so paltry a fashion.

It would have proved nothing,
living is the hardest miracle.

You always knew it was no longer possible;
beyond the betrayal dying is a trifle,
no longer an art to be perfected.
That has been mastered before.

Living is that shaft of sunlight
that does not enter my room any more.

It is costlier, I must confess
since passion through contracting breath
heaved the centre my days with you.

I offer you this for it includes
the deaths multifold without the dying,
without the respite to be dead
nor breathe the pretence of death.

A GIDDY MANNEQUIN

A giddy mannequin discreetly naked
I pose for you in a glass cage,
out of your reach, perfect and undefiled.

I learnt the use of facades
when you began destroying my porcelain dolls
so long treasured behind the purdah of my self.

Dead images and my mirrors in pieces
I strive to escape continually
the incarnation of my several selves
strewn casually over our encounters in time.

They glisten into life mocking me at multiple angles
as I puppet-dance to your discordant tunes.
I pretend not to take notice of such things.

Even this discerning unconcern
I stole from your eyes unaware,
perfected to an art of survival

As you, in perpetual ambush,
prefer to remove your glasses
before you come forward to splinter mine.

I have nothing to be sad about
as our images crackle and drag.
My body remains silent and complete,
a giddy mannequin discreetly naked.

NO LONGER DO I FRAME MYSELF

No longer do I frame myself in mirrors.
It is not as if I have finally gone beyond self-
adoration, nor is it that the glass cracks across
and my image aborts in a familiar nemesis.

It is only an emptiness whose depths disturb
the smooth surfaces of reality.

Soon you will be aware of absences,
I whisper in a crowd to the mirror
with receding memories of other presences
that grew beside me like trees,
colourless, dead with blighted leaves.

The branches mock my featurelessness.
Strange greeting for having accomplished
the ultimate miracle: complete effacement of self.

Steeled with the sheen of a glassy light,
the mirror continues with nonchalance its illusions.

Perfect, a white pillar of light,
I now float across mirrors
that once dared to catch me in multiple images.

FREED OF FASCINATION

Last night the blizzard trapped us all.
Those who built the snowman in our square
renounced the sky to its antics after all these years.
Thirty one, the weatherman last reported.

And I was grateful spared of such annunciation
trying to depart passionless through the door of the sun.
I awoke that pristine morning to my landscape
completely altered in anticipation of your coming.

You too had once arrived, unannounced,
ushering in ecstasy into my ivory singleness
with the candid breath of syllables:
Let's do it properly.
It snowed properly for days without end.

Our world surpassed all fulfilment of beauty
until the snowstorm trapped us all.
After all these years not to be freed of fascination
meant that loving had mostly to do with being human.

The delicate flakes hardened to ice before the thaw.
Strangers who slipped on the slush cursed as they fell,
curses that had nothing to do with loving or giving.

I too lived my days, equally vulnerable, unable to curse
knowing the sun will banish the snowman from my mandala.

FRIENDSHIP

(For a friend on moving into his new home)

> *Two people, yes, two lasting friends.*
> *The giving comes, the taking ends.*
> *There is no measure for such things.*
> *For this all Nature slows and sings.*
>   Elizabeth Jennings

"Happiness in your new home"
the card from the local newsagent's proclaims.
I insert every before happiness
hoping you will discover it all —
peace & contentment, freedom & joy, love & security —
in your new life, in your new home.
I exorcise your hearth like a pagan priestess.

I have treasured the gentle beam in your eyes,
the freedom of your soul soaring in your smile
for my happiness & riches, fame & fortune are measured by these.

You want me as a friend, you said.
You are the most precious gift in my life, I acknowledge.
Friend, lover, husband: a bond I know not how to split.

There is no insurance to protect me from losing you
except my prayers that all through eternity
you will grow to love me perfectly, bit by bit.

Our friendship is destined to be
more than a passing shelter in a storm.

Now that you are moving into your new home,
I wish you many happy beginnings;
your emotional landscape no longer shrouded
with remembrances of lives long past.

I listen to our frozen and unplayed music,
yearning for the thaw to loosen us forward,
unleash the passions we both trust and respect in us
like the voices of our dream children echoing
in our garden along with those of our parents.

Our friendship pure like the light of day,
clear of our past, prepared for a radiant future.
I need you, my friend, free-spirited like the lark
in the open sky, celebrating its mastery of nature.

PYREXIA OF UNKNOWN ORIGIN

The sky is one blank, silver-grey scroll
from my bed in the Princess Grace Hospital;
perfect setting for a late afternoon meditation
as I lie with a fever of unknown origin.

I imagine the maples in Westonbirt arboretum
as they gracefully conduct an autumnal sonata
proudly displaying their magnificent foliage.
This season I have missed my annual pilgrimage.

The moon shines directly on my face as I
awaken to an inky blue negative film of a sky
with the globe of a fully exposed moon
developing in cumulous clouds' cocoon.

I pile blankets on me measuring the speed of the moon
racing with the gypsy clouds in flight,
winking at me at the crossing of each rubicon;
when the passage is rough, the moon lies eclipsed.

Nurses and doctors come and go, taking my temperature,
blood pressure, samples of urine and blood for culture;
chest X-ray, abdominal scan, endoscopy, tests galore.
I lie exhausted, waiting for the phone to ring.

I wait for you like a bare, forked tree in winter
dreaming of spring, for buds and leaves to appear;
this need to live with you like an elixir
will cure my pyrexia of unknown origin.

WAITING

It is already too late for me to stem
the pain your silence has dredged up in me.
I search in your eyes for that flicker of belonging;
in your voice, a message I can read clearly that we,
without any doubt, belong to each other, and that nothing
else counts, the possession of our love a guaranteed gem.

But love does not stoop to offer such warranty.
I falter, not trusting myself for I am too far gone;
always losing those I love, now a habit with me!
Our kaleidoscopic friendship, from where love was born,
gently rearranges us and the stars of our destiny.
My mother prays to alter my karma with her puja's bounty,

Hoping to find me finely balanced and not lacking;
wanting me to have all that had been denied to her.
My consolation lies in the distance between us
for a daughter cannot bear to see her mother suffer.
Love that can be shared and passed around is
what will survive this fragile frame's passing.

What more can I offer to you that I have not already ?
Four postcards in ten days from Italy was a surfeit
of my love. One would have been fine! Were you serious ?
Loving in homeopathic doses is also a kind of conceit;
why do you need even one postcard, phone call or kiss ?
I will wait silently for your coming when you are ready.

TREES

Strange fetish of trees in the snow;
so many pagodas their arches seem,
consecrating the ground they half bury themselves in.

The fog meditates on ivory stupas,
revealing no passion only the landscape's anonymity.

Eyes under purdah see what lies are meant for
knowing no adultery, no abortion, no self-obsession,
meeting the protocol of seasons effortlessly.
Charismatic ambassadors, leaves negotiate with the sun.

In this they are not trapped philomels,
their peplus offers no autobiography.
Freed of self portraits, they do their vanishing mime
with the singleness of yoginis renouncing the act.

FORGETTING

Forgetting is like wintering here,
a lonely preoccupation.

The assiduity of mists
learning to balance
on moving shadows of sunshine
is what tired eyelids close upon.

Awareness is restful
though seeing is fatiguing.

Squinting of eyes dazzled
by light on snowscape is merciful.
Seeing, though free, is dear to negotiate.

The sunshine is excitable too,
forgetting it is white winter still,
offering in its shafts golden amnesia.

FOR THE DISPOSSESSED

Each passion in my sinews' landscape
strives to encounter itself articulate.
Consciousness is captivity, held in silence.

So have you recreated my womanhood
in the tradition of whoring goddesses
treading this cultured sunshine
in a processional of marionettes.

Nor am I exactly my self-conferred queen.
I cannot even define this becoming.
These syllables are familiar to me.
Here is my space, but I cannot lie in it.

Then I must speak for the dispossessed
for the exploration is no longer the same.

WORDS AS PLACES

Images of retreating words
mirage our unexplored thoughts,
travellers in an alien country,
unprotected self-portraits.

The images come straight through the masquerade
from the bottom of this immense pool of seeming.
This the defect of our too great nearness,
attributing to one experiences of the other.

I can only have my own awareness of you,
a ritual out of myself I must provide for.

You pinned all your metaphors on me,
ferocious alphabets sprawled upon my limbs.

Anywhere I grow, I have to find a place elsewhere.
The landscape alters irrevocably with my coming.
I cannot have knowledge of it before my coming.

EYES UNREAL

*The dew's disadvantage
in a multiple light
is that eyes are born in the flower.*
                    Pablo Neruda

The unavoidable accompaniment
of the morning's ascent
are multiple fibre dreams
congealed in a dimensionless light
when eyes unreal are born in me.

So many suns my floral corneas seem
quite uncentred still with such a windfall;
sudden escarpment of vision.

Dews that balance on my bespeckled
surface are borne along with
my new awareness of a self.

They are minuscule orbs no longer
but so many golden mandalas
that into my vortices draw the world.

Argus-eyed, I contemplate the universe.

Even such revelation transpires
as the look in these metaphors
reflect the illusion of being looked upon.

Depart passionless through the door of the sun.

Mundaka Upanishad